Microsoft Visio 2013 Advanced

Michelle N. Halsey

ISBN-10: 1-64004-150-8

ISBN-13: 978-1-64004-150-9

Silver City Publications & Training, L.L.C.
P.O. Box 1914
Nampa, ID 83653
https://www.silvercitypublications.com/shop/

Contents

Chapter 1 – Exploring Advanced Diagrams

This chapter will provide the groundwork in some basic Visio terms before you start learning the procedures related to those terms. We'll also create some drawings based on Visio templates: a calendar, a map, a flowchart, and an organization chart. You'll also learn how to use perspective drawings.

Understanding Visio Definitions

- A **Drawing** is the same as a File in Visio. The drawing contains all of the elements that come together to help others visualize your idea. A drawing can contain multiple pages. It stores the stencils used on those pages.

- **Pages** are just like pages in any other application. The point to remember is that drawings can contain multiple pages.

- **Layers** work together to make up a page. We'll talk in more details about layers later in the course. For now, just remember that each page can have multiple layers, and different pages of a drawing can have different sets of layers.

- **Shapes** are the objects in your drawing, whether one dimensional (lines) or two dimensional.

- **Stencils** are containers for your shapes. Stencils don't do anything except store related shapes for easy access. You can have multiple stencils that you use in a drawing, including stencils you create.

- **Templates** are the Visio starter drawings that include common stencils and shapes needed for that kind of drawing. They may also include layers to help you organize your drawing.

Creating Calendars

Use the following procedure to create a daily calendar in Visio:

Step 1; Select the File tab to open the Backstage View.

Step 2: Select New.

Step 3: Select the Schedule Template Category.

Step 4: Select Calendar.

Step 5: Select the measurement units.

Step 6: Select Create.

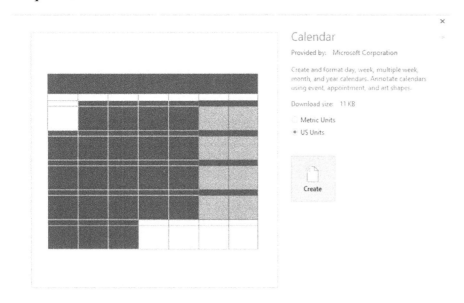

Take a look at the different shapes available in the Calendar template.

Shapes

STENCILS   SEARCH

More Shapes ▶

Quick Shapes

Calendar Shapes

Month		Week	
Multiple week		Thumbnail month	
Year		Day	
Appointment		Multi-day event	
Clock		Note	
Reminder		Important	
Meeting		Pushpin	
Attention		Idea	
Travel-air		Travel-train	
Travel-car		Travel-ship	
Special event		Vacation	
Celebration		Birthday	
Sports		Anniversary	

Drag a day, week, month, and appointment shape to the drawing one at a time and investigate the configuration options with each shape.

Step 1: Drag appointment to canvas.

Step 2: Right-click and select Configure to open the Configure window.

Step 3: Enter the Configure settings.

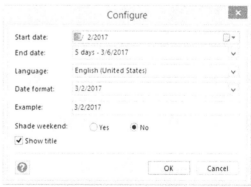

 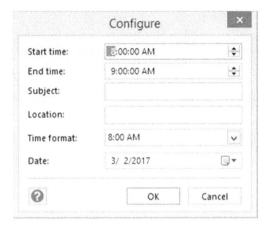

Creating Maps

Use the following procedure to create a directional map:

Step 1: Select the File tab to open the Backstage View.

Step 2: Select New.

Step 3: Select the Maps and Floor plans Template Category.

Step 4: Select Directional map.

Step 5: Select the measurement units.

Step 6: Select Create.

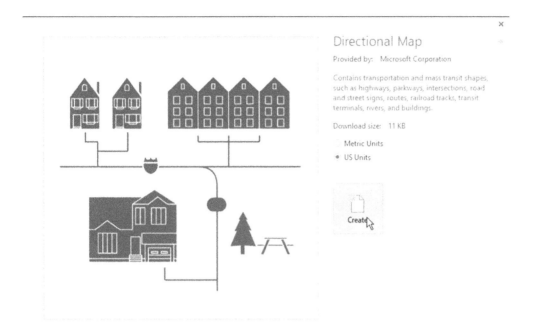

Take a look at the different shapes available in the map template, including the Metro, Recreation, Transportation, and Road categories.

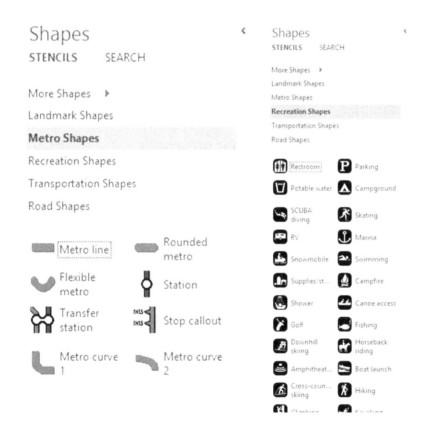

Drag shapes to the drawing to create your map.

Flowcharts Shapes

The following flowchart shapes are available:

- Use the **Terminator** shape for the first and last step of your process.

- Use the **Process** shape to represent a step in your process.

- Use the **Predefined process** shape for a set of steps that combine to create a sub-process defined on another page of the drawing.

- Use the **Decision** shape to indicate a point where the outcome of a decision dictates the next step. Although you can use multiple outcomes, often there are just two —yes and no.

- Use the **Document** shape to represent a step that results in a document.

- Use the **Data** shape to indicate information coming into the process from outside, or leaving the process. This shape can also be used to represent materials and is sometimes called an Input/Output shape.

- The **Flowchart** shape can be interchanged between Process, Decision, Document, or Data. Any text you type onto the shape, or information you add to its Shape Data, remains with the shape. Right-click to change the shape.

- Use the **Stored data** shape for a step that results in information being stored.

- Use the **On-page reference** shape to indicate that the next (or previous) step is somewhere else on the drawing. This is great for large flowcharts where you would otherwise have to use a long connector, which can be hard to follow.

- Use the **Off-page reference** shape to create a set of hyperlinks between two pages.

- Use the **Dynamic connector** to draw a path around other shapes.

- Use the **Line-curve connector** when you need adjustable curvature in your connector between shapes.

- Use the **Auto-height box** for a text box that adjusts to accommodate your text. You can set the width by dragging the sides.

- Use the **Annotation** shape for a bracketed text box to add comments about your flowchart shapes.

- Use the **Manual input** shape to show a step where a person provides information to the process.

- Use the **Manual operation** shape to show a step that must be performed by a person.

- Use the **Internal storage** shape to represent information stored on a computer.

- Use the **Direct data** shape to represent information stored so that any single record can be accessed directly. This represents how a computer hard-drive stores data.

- Use the **Sequential data** shape to represent information stored in sequence, such as data on a magnetic tape. When data is stored in sequence, it must be retrieved in sequence.

- Use the **Card and Paper tape** shape to represent a physical card or paper tape. Early computer systems used a system of punch cards and paper tape to store and retrieve data and to store and run programs.

- Use the **Display** shape to represent information that is displayed to a person, usually on a computer screen.

- Use the **Preparation** shape to indicate where variables are initialized in preparation for a procedure.

- Use the **Parallel** mode shape to show where two different processes can operate simultaneously.

- Use the **Loop** limit shape to mark the maximum number of times a loop can run before it must go on to the next step.

- Use the **Control** transfer shape to indicate a step that goes to a step other than the typical next step when certain conditions are met.

Use the following procedure to create a flowchart:

Step 1: Select the File tab to open the Backstage View.

Step 2: Select New.

Step 3: Select the Flowchart Template Category.

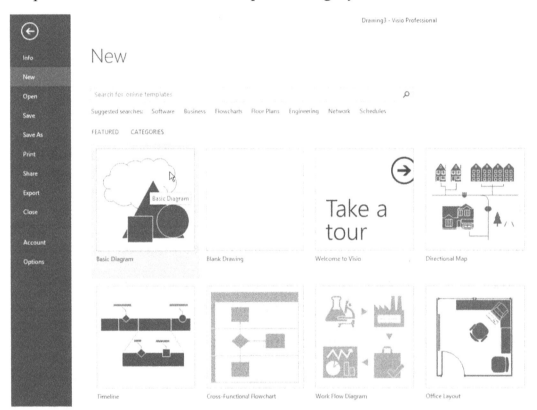

Step 4: Select Basic Flowchart.

Step 5: Select the measurement units.

Step 6: Select Create.

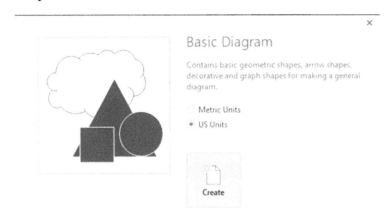

Take a look at the different shapes available in the flowchart template.

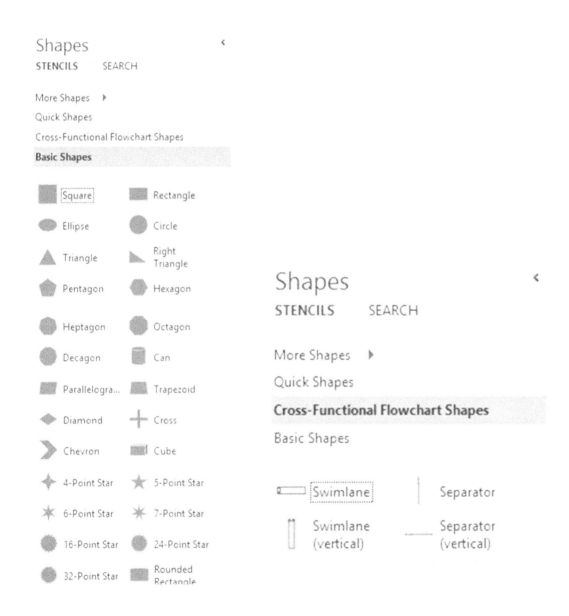

Drag shapes to the drawing to create your flowchart. You can use the connector tool on the Tools area of the Home tab on the Ribbon. Drag from a connection point on the first shape to a connection point on the second shape.

Creating Organization Charts

Use the following procedure to create an organization chart:

Step 1: Select the File tab to open the Backstage View.

Step 2: Select New.

Step 3: Search for Organization Chart.

Step 4: Select Organization Chart.

Step 5: Select the measurement units.

Step 6: Select Create.

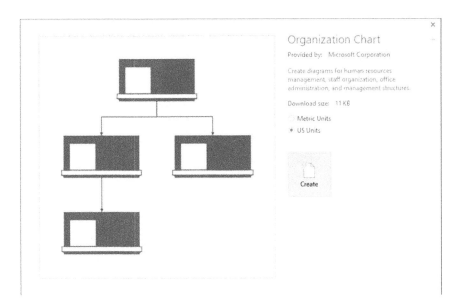

Take a look at the different shapes available in the flowchart template.

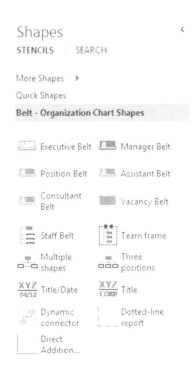

Drag shapes to the drawing to create your organization. Enter the information you want to include about each position or person in the box. To show a subordinate to that position, drag the next shape on top of it to automatically connect it.

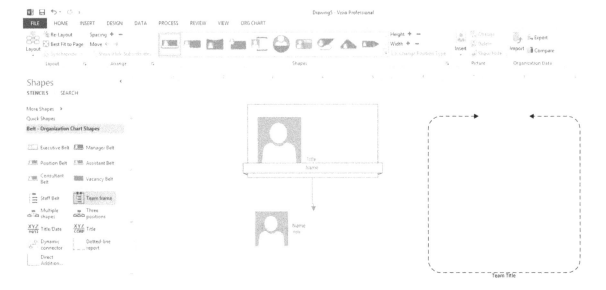

Using Perspective

Use the following procedure to create a block diagram with perspective:

Step 1: Select the File tab to open the Backstage View.

Step 2: Select New.

Step 3: Search for Block Diagram with Perspective.

Step 4: Select Block Diagram with Perspective.

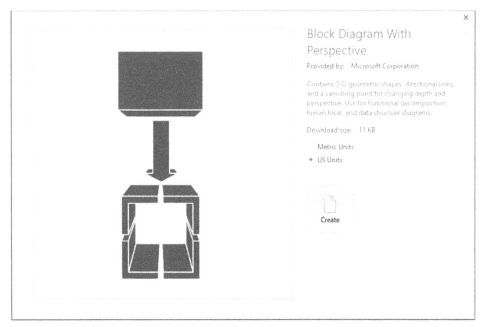

Step 5: Drag the Blocks with Perspective shapes onto the drawing.

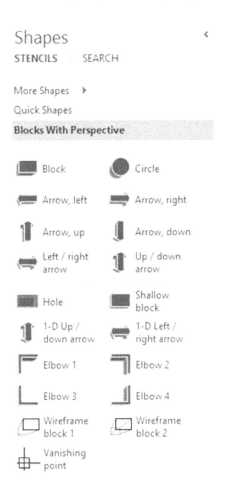

Step 6: To change the perspective of a shape, drag the vanishing point (marked VP) to a new location.

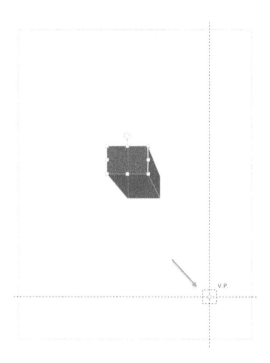

Step 7: To set the depth of a shape, right-click the shape you want to change and select Set Depth from the context menu.

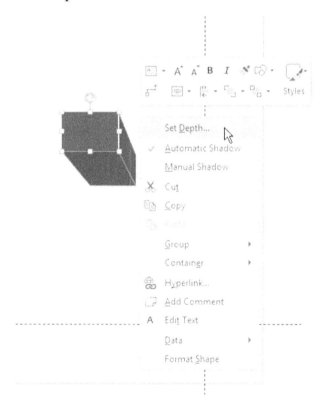

Step 8: Select the Depth from the drop down list and select OK.

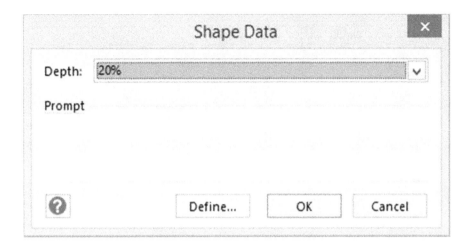

Network Diagrams

Use the following procedure to create a network diagram:

Step 1: Select the File tab to open the Backstage View.

Step 2: Select New.

Step 3: Search for Network Diagram.

Step 4: Select Basic Network Diagram.

Step 5: Select the measurement units.

Step 6: Select Create.

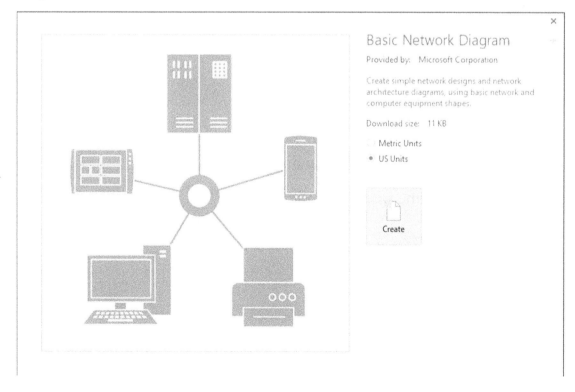

Take a look at the different shapes available in the network diagram template.

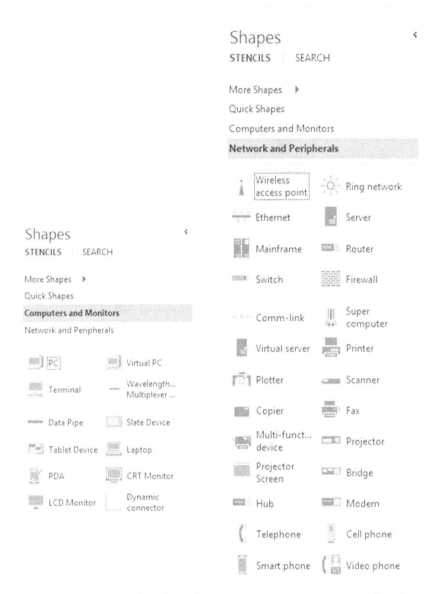

Drag shapes to the drawing to create your network diagram.

Marketing Diagrams

Use the following procedure to create a marketing diagram:

Step 1: Select the File tab to open the Backstage View.

Step 2: Select New.

Step 3: Search for Marketing Charts and Diagrams.

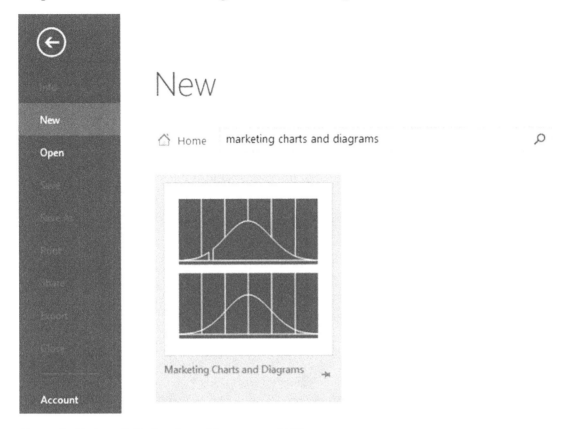

Step 4: Select Marketing Charts and Diagrams.

Step 5: Select the measurement units.

Step 6: Select Create.

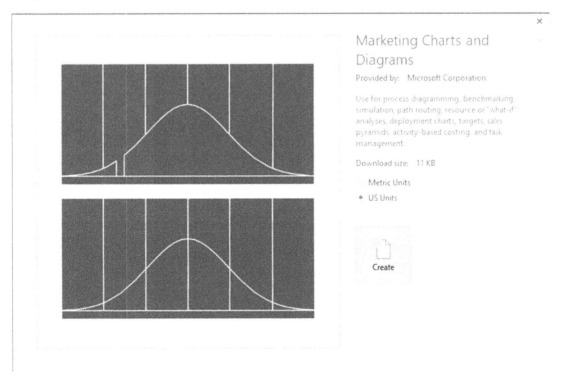

Take a look at the different shapes available in the marketing charts and diagram template.

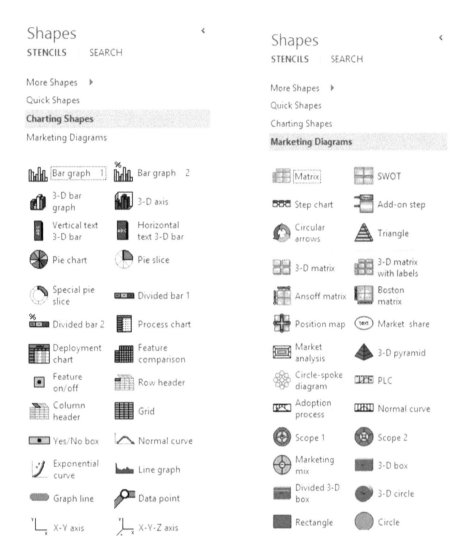

Drag shapes to the drawing to create your marketing diagram.

Create Work Flow Diagrams

Use the following procedure to create a work flow diagram:

Step 1: Select the File tab to open the Backstage View.

Step 2: Select New.

Step 3: Search for Flow Chart.

Step 4: Select Work Flow Diagram.

Step 5: Select the measurement units.

Step 6: Select Create.

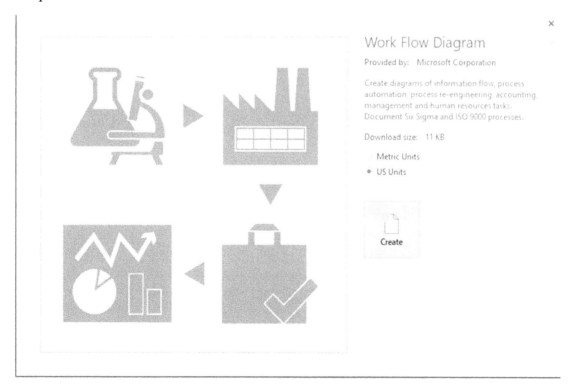

Take a look at the different shapes available in the Work Flow Diagram template. Use the scroll bar to see additional categories in the Shapes window.

Create Fishbone (Cause and Effect) Diagrams

Use the following procedure to create a cause and effect diagram:

Step 1: Select the File tab to open the Backstage View.

Step 2: Select New.

Step 3: Search for Cause and Effect Diagram.

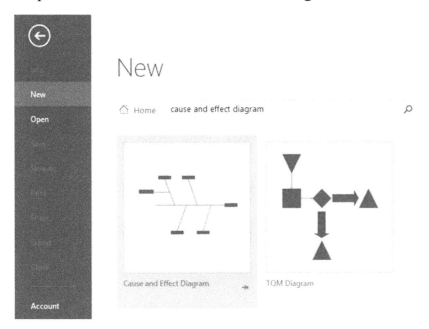

Step 4: Select Cause and Effect Diagram.

Step 5: Select the measurement units.

Step 6: Select Create.

Take a look at the different shapes available in the Cause and Effect Diagram template.

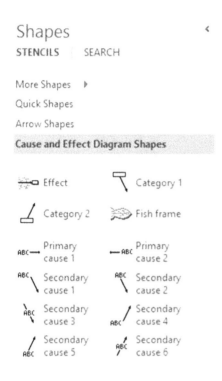

Step 7: On the drawing, select the spine and type text to describe the effect, problem, or objective.

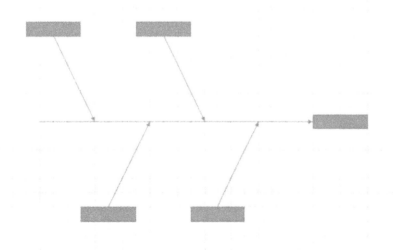

Step 8: Drag shapes to the drawing and position accordingly.

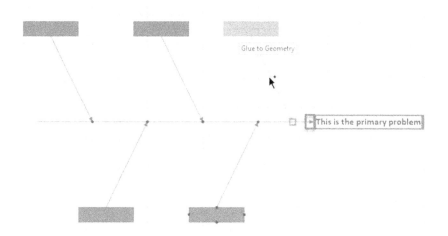

You can label the shapes, include primary and secondary cause shapes, and even rotate or flip shapes.

Project Management Diagrams

Use the following procedure to use the sample project management diagram:

Step 1: Select the File tab to open the Backstage View.

Step 2: Select New.

Step 3: Search for Pivot Diagram.

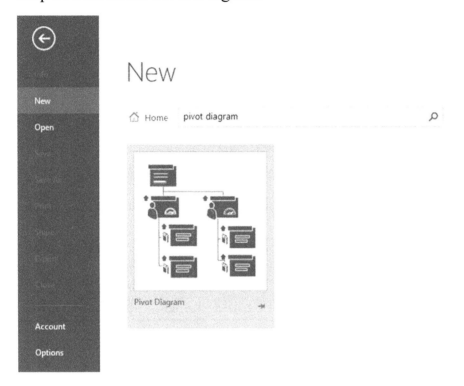

Step 4: Select Pivot Diagram.

Step 5: Select the measurement units.

Step 6: Select Create.

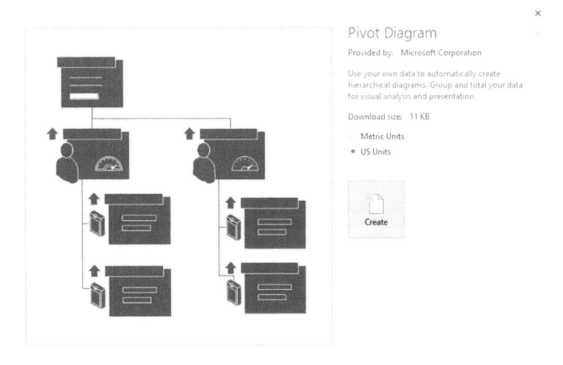

Step 7: Select the Data Source you want to use and then click Next.

Take a look at the different shapes available in the Pivot Diagram template.

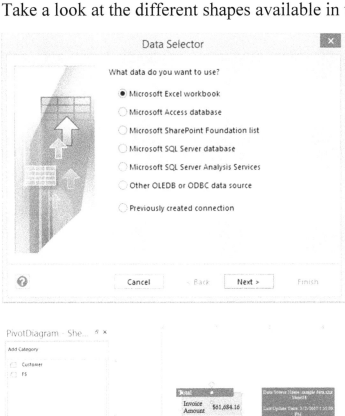

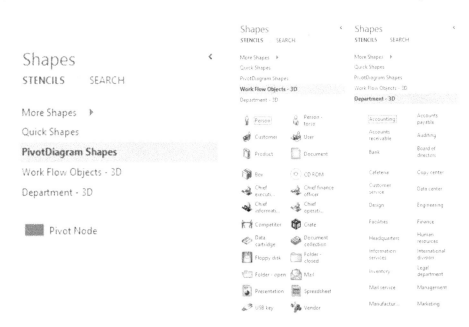

Gantt Charts

Use the following procedure to create a Gantt chart:

Step 1: Select the File tab to open the Backstage View.

Step 2: Select New.

Step 3: Search for Gantt Chart.

Step 4: Select Gantt Chart.

Step 5: Select the measurement units.

Step 6: Select Create.

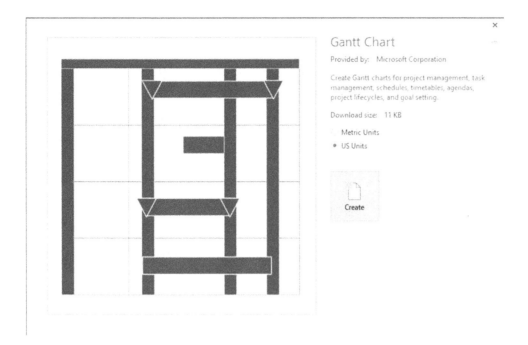

Visio displays the Gant Chart Options dialog box.

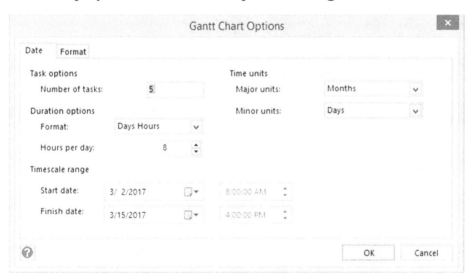

Step 7: Enter the Number of Tasks you want to represent on the chart. Enter the Time Units, Duration Options, and Timescale Range information.

Step 8: Review the options on the Format tab.

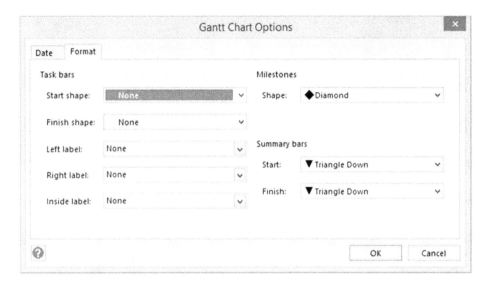

Step 9: Select OK.

Review your Gantt chart. Make changes in the fields as appropriate.

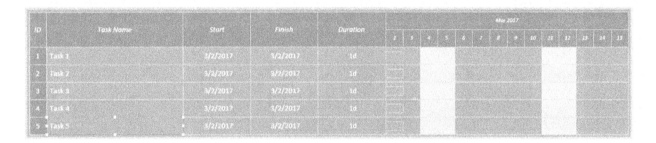

Take a look at the different shapes available in the Gantt Chart template.

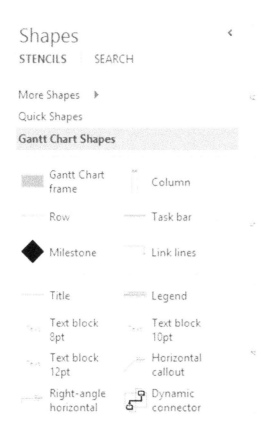

Review the Tools on the Gantt Chart tab of the Ribbon.

Hover the mouse over the tools to see screen tips.

PERT Charts

Use the following procedure to create a PERT chart:

Step 1: Select the File tab to open the Backstage View.

Step 2: Select New.

Step 3: Search for PERT chart.

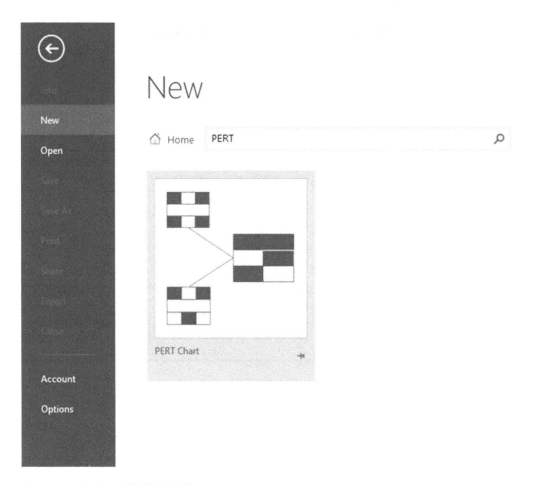

Step 4: Select PERT Chart.

Step 5: Select the measurement units.

Step 6: Select Create.

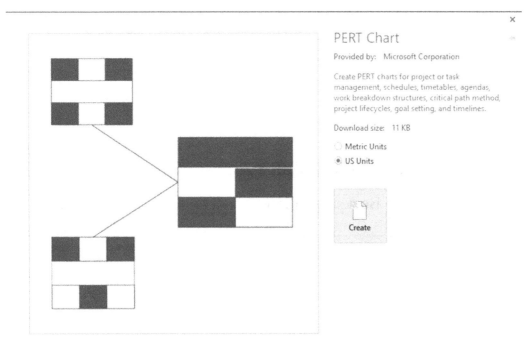

Take a look at the different shapes available in the PERT Chart template.

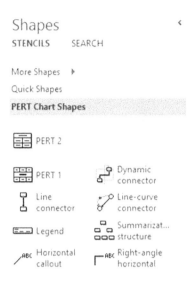

Drag shapes to the drawing to create your chart. The default text is only meant to guide you in your chart creation. You can select it to replace it with appropriate text.

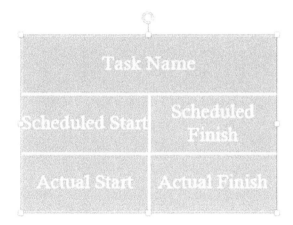

Chapter 2 – Working with Stencils and Shapes

This chapter will explain how to work with stencils. Remember that stencils are containers for shapes. First, we'll look at how to create and save a custom stencil. Then you'll learn how to add shapes to the stencil from other drawings or other stencils. Finally, we'll look at the controlling shape placement on your drawings using the Snap & Glue tools.

Creating Custom Stencils

Use the following procedure to create a custom stencil:

Step 1: Select the More Shapes option in the Shapes window. Select New Stencil.

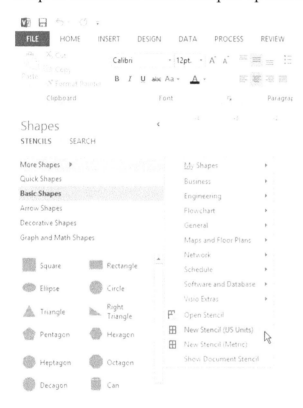

Adding Shapes to the Stencil

Use the following procedure to add a shape to a stencil:

Step 1: Open the stencil where the shape you want to add will be stored. For this example, use the Favorites. Select More Shapes from the Shapes window. Select My Shapes. Select Favorites.

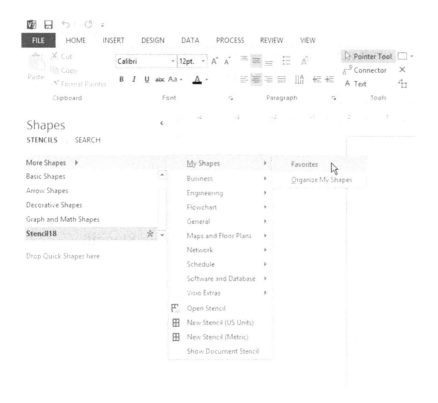

Step 2: Make sure that the stencil is editable by right-clicking the stencil title bar and select Edit Stencil from the context menu.

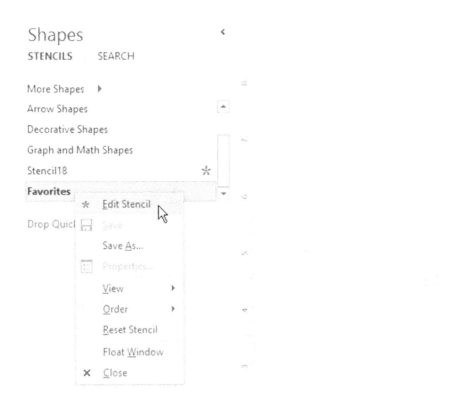

Step 3: Select the shape that you want to add to the stencil from the drawing page.

Step 4: To copy the shape, press the CTRL key while you drag the shape to the stencil.

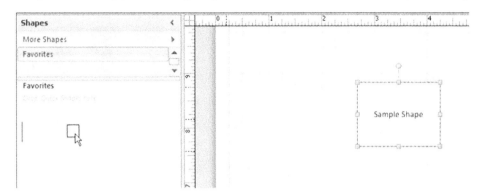

Step 5: The icon on the stencil is labeled as Master X, where X is a number corresponding to the number of shapes you have copied.

Use the following procedure to copy a shape from one stencil to another:

Step 1: Open the stencil that contains the shape you want to copy.

Step 2: Right click the shape that you want to copy and select **Add to My Shapes.** Select the stencil where you want to copy the shape.

Saving the Stencil

Use the following procedure to save a stencil and save a copy of a stencil:

Step 1: Select the Save icon on the stencil title bar.

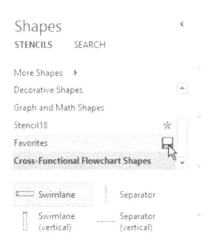

Step 2: To save a copy of the stencil, right-click the stencil title bar and select **Save As** from the context menu. Enter a name for the new stencil and select **Save**.

Controlling Shape Placement

Use the following procedure to snap shapes into position:

Step 1: Select the **View** tab from the Ribbon.

Step 2: Select the small square next to the Visual Aids group to open the Snap & Glue dialog box.

Step 3: Under Snap To, check the boxes to indicate which items you want to use when snapping shapes. These settings apply to all shapes in the drawing.

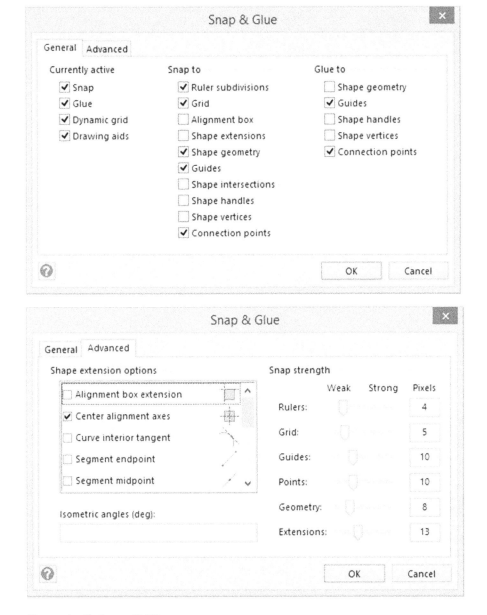

Step 4: Select **OK**.

Chapter 3 – Advanced Custom Shape Design

This chapter will explain the tools you need to customize shapes. We'll start with learning about the Quick Shapes area of the Shapes window. You'll learn how to create your own shapes and revise existing shapes. We'll also take a look at how to lock and protect shapes so that they won't get changed accidentally.

Using Quick Shapes

The Quick Shapes area is at the top of a stencil. Notice the thin divider between the Quick Shapes and the other shapes in that stencil.

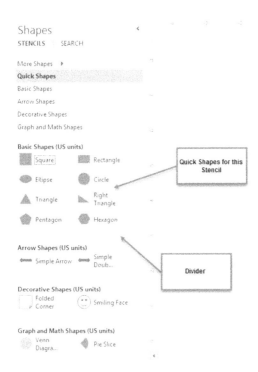

The following diagram shows the Quick Shapes stencil. In this example, there are three stencils open.

Note that the Quick Shape area allows you to use a few shapes from each stencil you have open. In this way, you won't have to switch between stencils as you work with your most used shapes.

Use the following procedure to move a frequently used shape to the Quick Shapes area of the stencil.

Step 1: Drag the Shape from the bottom part of the Stencil window to the top of that stencil. A small icon for the shape, plus a thin vertical bar shows where the shape will be placed in the Quick Shapes area.

Note that you can use this same method to rearrange the order of the shapes in the stencil.

Now take another look at the Quick Shapes stencil. The shape you added to Quick Shapes in the Basic Shapes stencil is now shown in the Quick Shapes stencil.

Creating New Shapes

To create a shape on your Favorites stencil. Use the following procedure.

Step 1: To open the stencil where you want to store the new shape, select More Shapes from the Shapes window. Select My Shapes. Select Favorites or the name of your custom stencil.

Step 3: Right-click the stencil title bar and select Edit Stencil from the context menu. The icon in the title bar changes to show that the stencil is editable.

Step 2: Right-click the stencil window and select New Master from the context menu.

Step 4: Enter a Name for shape in the New Master dialog box.

Step 5: Enter a Prompt if desired.

Step 6: Select an Icon size to show on the stencil for the custom shape.

Step 7: Select Left, Center, or Right as the alignment.

Step 8: Check the Match master by name on drop box if desired.

Step 9: Check the Generate icon automatically from shape data box if desired.

Step 10: Select OK.

Step 11: Right-click the new blank shape icon in the stencil and select Edit Master from the context menu. Select Edit Master Shape.

Step 12: Visio opens a blank canvas for you to design the shape. You can draw the shape just as you can on a regular drawing page, using different stencil shapes, drawing using the drawing tools or pasting objects from another application.

Step 13: When you have finished drawing the shape, close the custom shape drawing window. Visio displays a dialog box asking if you want to save the changes to the shape. Select Yes.

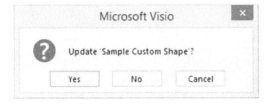

Step 13: Remember to Save your stencil.

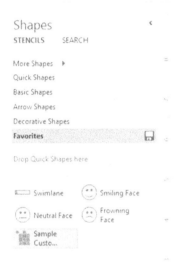

Revising Existing Shapes

Use the following procedure to edit a shape on a stencil:

Step 1: Open the stencil where the shape you want to edit is stored.

Step 2: If the stencil you opened is not editable, right-click the stencil title bar and select Edit Stencil from the context menu. The icon in the title bar changes to show that the stencil is editable.

Step 3: Right-click the stencil window and select Edit Master Shape from the context menu.

Step 4: Visio opens a separate canvas for you to edit the shape. You can use different stencil shapes, the drawing tools or pasted objects from another application.

Step 5: When you have finished drawing the shape, close the custom shape drawing window. Visio displays a dialog box asking if you want to save the changes to the shape. Select Yes.

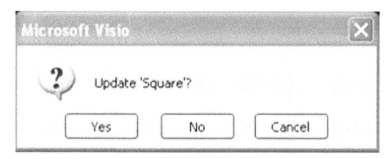

Step 6: Remember to Save your stencil.

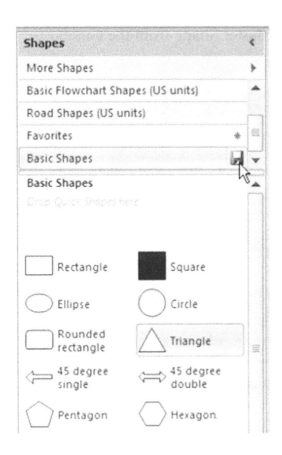

Locking and Protecting Shapes

Use the following procedure to display the Developer tab:

Step 1: Select the File tab to open the Backstage View.

Step 2: Select Options.

Step 3: Select the Advanced category.

Step 4: Scroll down to the General section.

Step 5: Check the Run in Developer mode box.

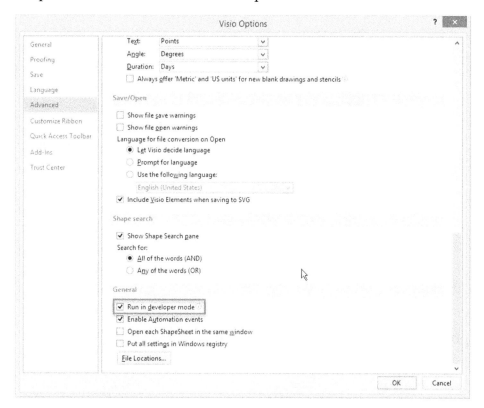

Step 6: Select OK.

Step 7: Select the Developer tab.

Use the following procedure to protect a shape:

Step 1: Select the shape you want to protect.

Step 2: Select Protection from the Shape Design group on the Developer tab on the Ribbon.

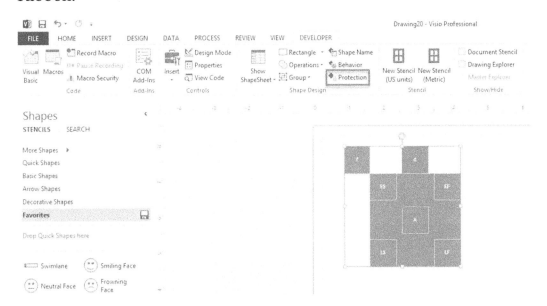

Step 3: Check the boxes to protect one or more of the following attributes of the selected shape.

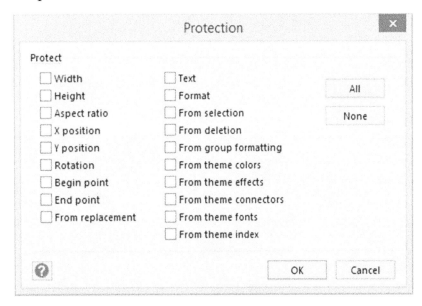

Step 4: Select OK.

Use the following procedure to lock a shape:

Step 1: Select the shape you want to protect.

Step 2: Select Protection from the Shape Design group on the Developer tab on the Ribbon.

Step 3: Check the From selection box.

Step 4: Select OK.

Step 5: Visio displays the Protection dialog box. Select OK to continue.

Step 6: Select Drawing Explorer from the Show/Hide group on the Developer tab of the Ribbon.

Step 7: Right-click the name of the drawing and select Protect Document from the context menu.

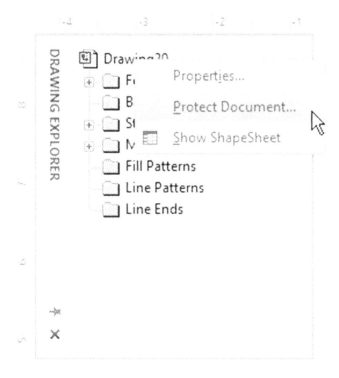

Step 8: Check the Shapes box to protect shapes from selection. Select OK.

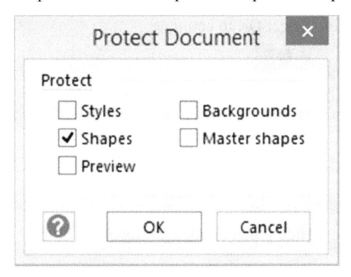

Chapter 4 – Layers

This chapter goes into how to use layers in Visio. You'll get an overview of layers, as well as learn how to create, remove, and rename layers. You'll also learn how to set layer properties and control shape placement. What if shapes were assigned to the wrong layer? You'll learn how to assign shapes to a new layer. You'll also learn how to assign color to a layer and will explain how to protect a layer from changes once you have it just like you want it. Finally, we'll look at how to print just the layers you want – one or more or all layers.

Understanding Layers

Layers are like have a drawing with multiple transparencies sitting on top of it. Each transparency shows a different aspect of the drawing. Using this concept, you can view or work with different layers at different times. Or you can view all of the layers together.

Imagine that you are drawing an office layout. You could place the walls, doors, and windows on one layer. The electrical outlets could be on a separate layer. Then put the furniture on a third layer. You could lock the other two layers while you work with the shapes in the electrical system. That will keep you from accidentally moving the walls or furniture.

The Layer Properties Dialog Box

The Layer Properties dialog box.

Step 1: Select Layer from the Editing group on the Home tab of the Ribbon.

Step 2: Select Layer Properties from the Layers drop down list to open the Layer Properties dialog box.

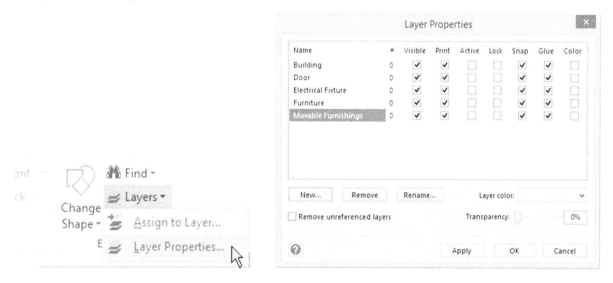

Working with Existing Layers

Use the following procedure to select shapes by layer:

Step 1: Choose the Select tool from the Home tab of the Ribbon. Choose Select by Type.

Step 2: In the Select by Type dialog box, select the Layer option.

Step 3: Check one or more boxes to indicate which layers' shapes you want to select. Only the layers that are currently displayed are available.

Step 4: Select OK.

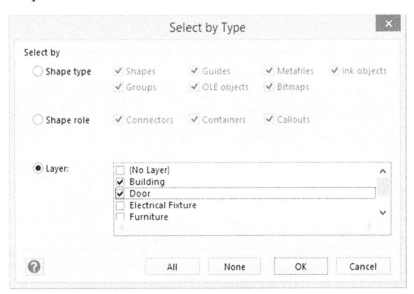

Visio shows the selected shapes on the currently displayed layers.

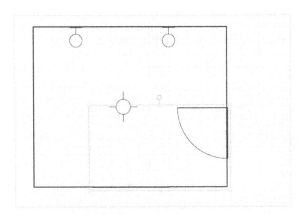

Hiding or Showing a Layer

Use the following procedure to hide a layer:

Step 1: Open the Layer Properties dialog box.

Step 2: Clear the Visible check box for any layer that you want to hide.

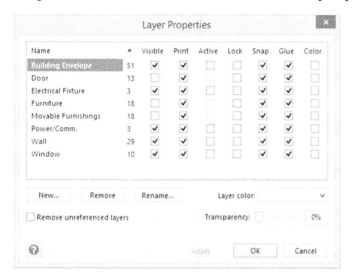

Step 3: Select OK.

Step 4: When you want to show the layers again, return to the Layer Properties dialog box and select the Visible checkbox next to the layers that you want to show.

Activating a Layer

Use the following procedure to activate a layer:

Step 1: Open the Layer Properties dialog box.

Step 2: Check the Active box next to any layers that you want to make active.

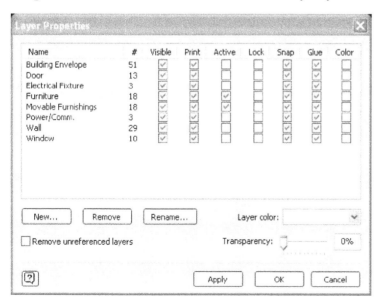

Creating Layers

Use the following procedure to add a layer:

Step 1: Open the Layer Properties dialog box.

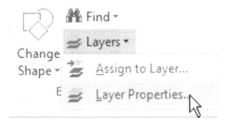

Step 2: Select New.

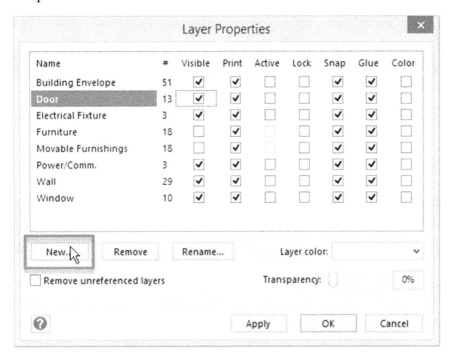

Step 3: Enter a name for your layer and select OK.

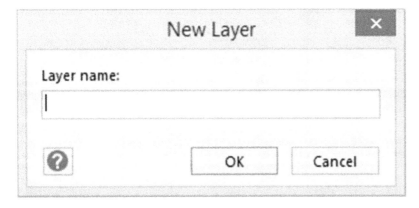

Step 4: Select OK in the Layer Properties dialog box.

Renaming and Removing Layers

Use the following procedure to rename a layer:

Step 1: Open the Layer Properties dialog box.

Step 2: Select the layer you want to rename.

Step 3: Select Rename.

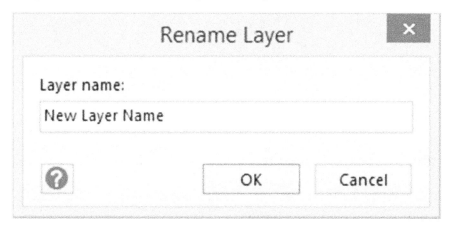

Step 4: In the Rename Layer dialog box, enter the new name and select OK.

Step 4: In the Layer Properties dialog box select OK.

Use the following procedure to delete a layer:

Step 1: Open the Layer Properties dialog box.

Step 2: Select the layer you want to remove.

Step 3: Select Remove.

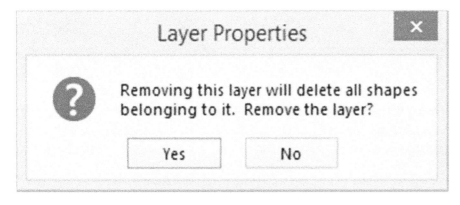

Step 4: If there are shapes on the selected layer, Visio displays the following message.

Step 5: Select Yes to continue.

Assigning Shapes to Layers

Use the following procedure to assign a shape to a layer:

Step 1: Select the shape on your drawing. You can assign more than one shape at a time by holding the CTRL key down while selecting the shapes.

Step 2: Select Layer from the Home tab on the Ribbon.

Step 3: Select Assign to Layer.

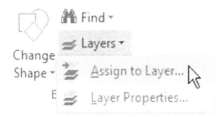

Step 4: On the Layer dialog box, check the boxes to indicate which layer(s) the shape should be assigned to. You can also select New to create a new layer and assign the shape at the same time.

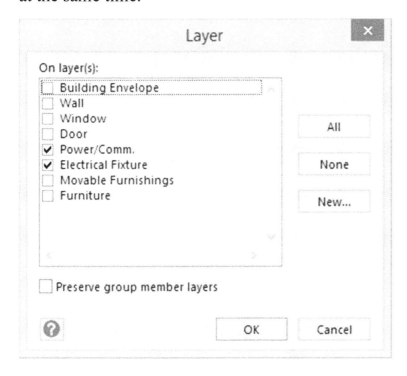

Assigning Color to a Layer

Use the following procedure to assign color to a layer:

Step 1: Open the Layer Properties dialog box.

Step 2: Select the layer you want to color.

Step 3: Select the Layer Color from the drop down list.

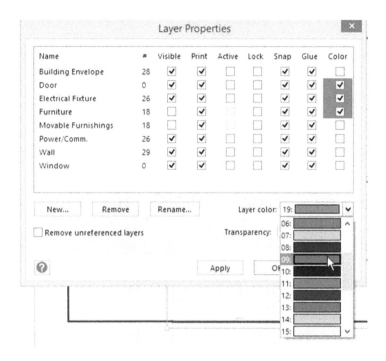

Step 4: To create a custom color, select More Colors from the Layer color drop down list.

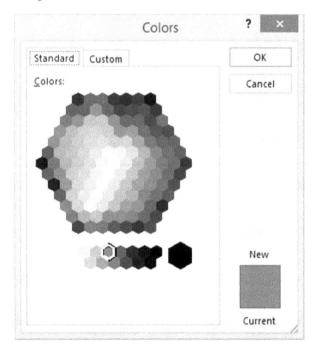

Step 5: Use the Colors dialog box to create your custom color and select OK.

Step 6: Select Apply.

Step 7: Select OK to close the Layer Properties dialog box.

Protecting a Layer from Changes

Use the following procedure to lock a layer:

Step 1: Open the Layer Properties dialog box.

Step 2: Check the Lock box next to any layers that you want to lock.

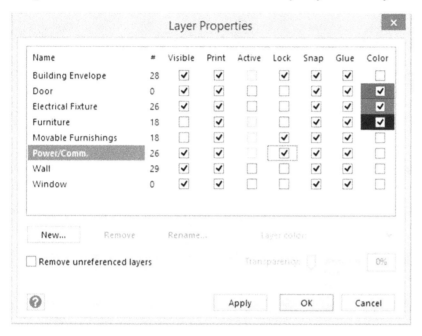

Printing Only the Layers You Want

Use the following procedure to print a layer:

Step 1: Open the Layer Properties dialog box.

Step 2: Check the Print box next to any layers that you want to print.

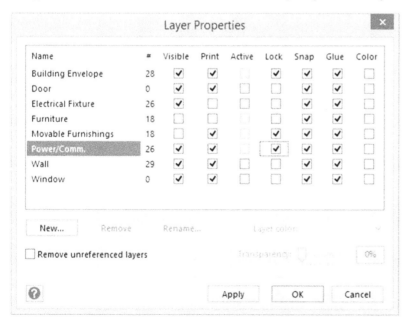

Chapter 5 – Multi-Page Drawings

In this chapter, you'll learn how to work with Visio pages. First, we'll look at how to add pages to a drawing. Then, you'll learn how to arrange pages. You'll also learn how to work with background pages. Finally, you'll learn how to use hyperlinks to navigate between multiple pages in your drawing.

Adding Pages to a Drawing

Use the following procedure to add a new page to a drawing:

Step 1: Select the Insert tab from the Ribbon.

Step 2: Select the Blank Page tool.

Step 3: Select Blank Page.

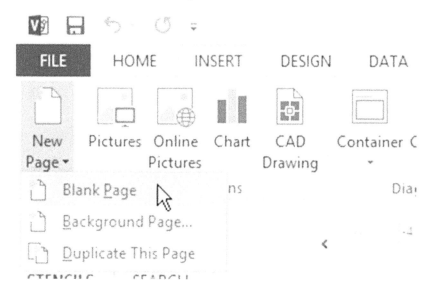

Visio adds a blank page with the same properties as the current page when you added the page.

You can also right-click the page tab at the bottom of the drawing window, and select Insert from the context menu.

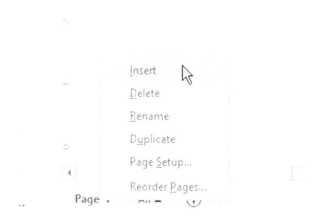

Visio opens the Page Setup dialog box, open to the Page Properties tab.

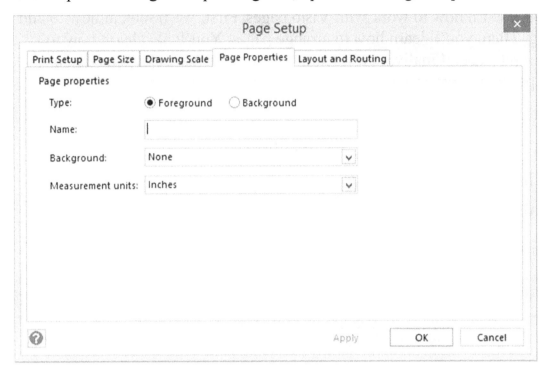

Step 1: Enter a Name for the page.

Step 2: If desired, select the Background page to apply to this page from the drop down list.

Step 3: Select the Measurement units from the drop down list.

Step 4: If you want to change other features of the page, use the Print Setup, Page Size, Drawing Scale, Layout and Routing, and Shadows tabs.

Step 5: Select OK.

Arranging Pages

Use the following procedure to reorder pages:

Step 1: Drag the page tabs into the new order.

Step 2: You can also right-click the page tab and select Reorder Pages from the context menu.

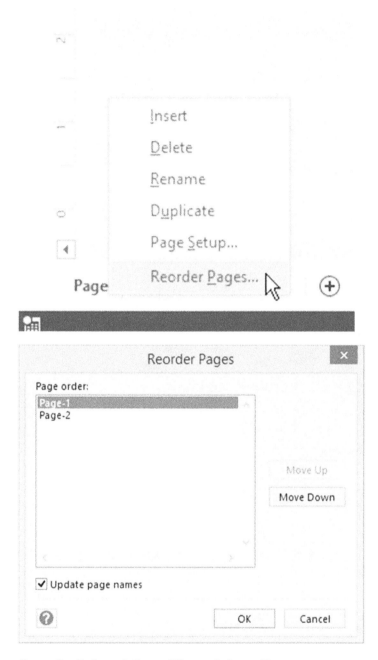

Step 3: Select Move Up or Move Down to rearrange the pages.

Step 4: Check the Update page names box if you want Visio to change the page names that include numbers.

Step 5: Select OK.

Working with Background Pages
Use the following procedure to add a background page:

Step 1: Select the Insert tab from the Ribbon.

Step 2: Select the Blank Page tool.

Step 3: Select Background Page. Or you can right-click a Page tab and select Insert from the context menu.

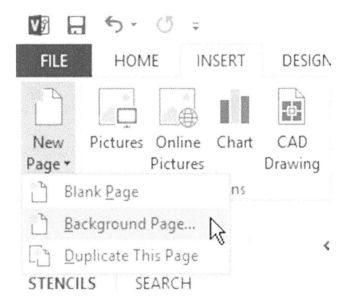

Step 4: In the Page Setup dialog box, select the Background option.

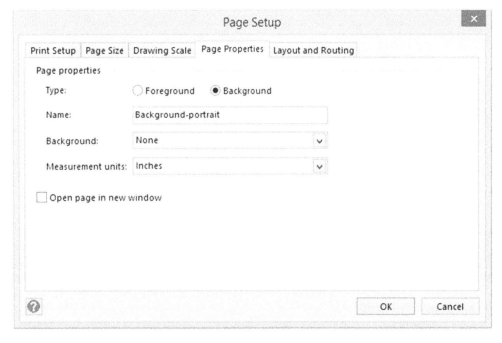

Step 5: Select OK.

Use the following procedure to assign a new background page to a page in a drawing:

Step 1: Right-click the Page tab for the page that you want to reassign.

Step 2: Select Page Setup from the context menu.

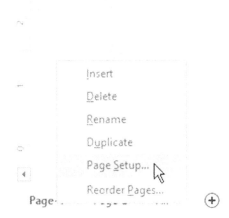

Step 3: On the Page Properties tab, select the new Background page from the drop down list.

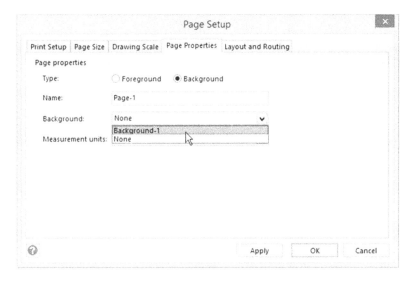

Step 4: Select Apply or OK.

Add shapes to the background page and then review the results on the pages that use that background page.

Hyperlinking Between Pages

Use the following procedure to add a hyperlink to another page in the drawing:

Step 1: Select the page or shape where you want to add the hyperlink.

Step 2: Select the Insert tab on the Ribbon.

Step 3: Select Hyperlink.

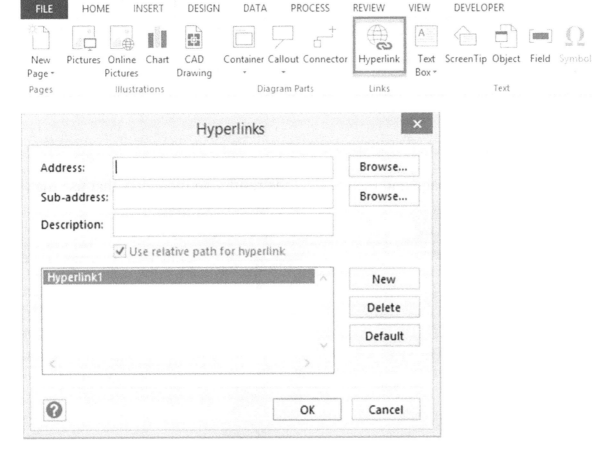

Step 4: Select Browse next to Address to locate the file you want to use, even though it is the same file.

Step 5: Select Local file

Step 6: Select the location of the current file and select Open.

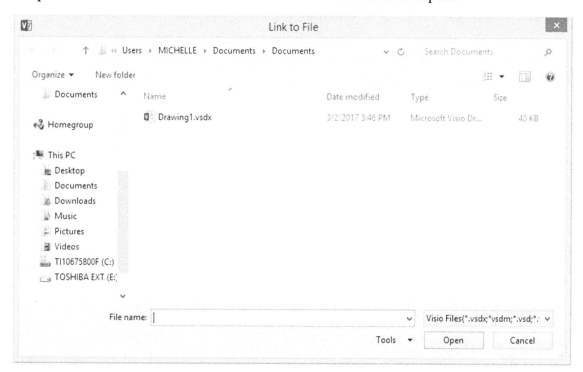

Step 7: Select Browse next to Sub-address to select the page.

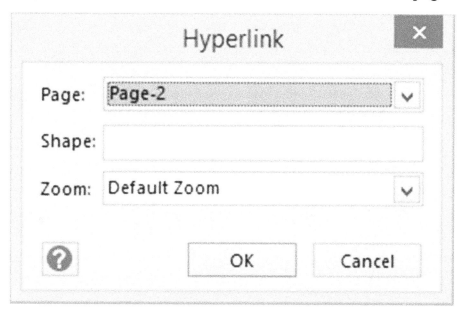

Step 8: Select the Page from the drop down list.

Step 9: Enter the Shape, if appropriate.

Step 10: Select the Zoom level from the drop down list.

Step 11: Select OK to close the dialog boxes.

When you hover the mouse over the link, the cursor shows that there is a link, as well as a screen tip for the link location. You can follow the link by pressing the Ctrl key while clicking the link or by right-clicking the shape and selecting the link from the context menu.

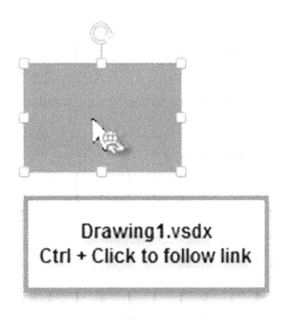

Chapter 6 – Creating Technical Layouts

This chapter explains how to draw with precision using the Size and Position window. We'll take a look at viewing area measurements for your shapes. You'll also learn how to set the drawing scale on your drawings. Finally, we'll work with building plan layouts to practice your drawing skills.

Drawing with Precision

The Size and Position dialog box. Use the following procedure.

Step 1: Select the View tab from the Ribbon.

Step 2: Select Task Panes.

Step 3: Select Size & Position Window.

Step 4: The Size and Position window opens in the bottom left corner of the screen.

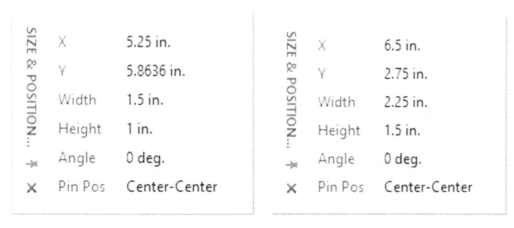

The Size and Position window shows different information, based on the type of shape you have selected. These examples show an arrow, a square, and a line. If different types of shapes are all selected, or nothing is selected, the window shows No Selection.

In each of the available fields, you can enter a precise measurement to get the shape exactly like you want it. You can also enter formulas, such as +1.5 ft. or -90 deg. This is helpful if you want to apply the same change to multiple similar shapes.

The Pin Position field controls where the "pin" on the shape that controls the rotation is located. You can select a new option from the drop down list.

Practice changing some of the Size and Position window measurements on their shapes to see the results.

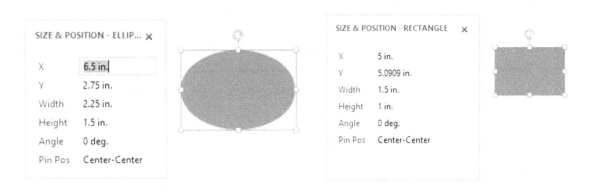

Setting a Drawing Scale

Use the following procedure to change the drawing scale:

Step 1: Display the page where you want a different drawing scale.

Step 2: Select the Design tab.

Step 3: Select the small square next to the Page Setup group.

Step 4: Select the Drawing Scale tab.

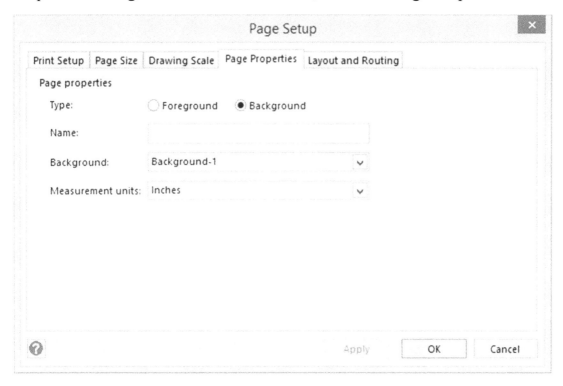

Step 5: Select Pre-defined scale and select a pre-defined type and scale from the drop down lists. Or select Custom scale and enter the scale.

Step 6: To change the measurement units, select the Page Properties tab.

Step 7: Select the new Measurement units from the drop down list.

Step 8: Select Apply to save your changes.

The drawing shows the new settings. Shapes might appear larger or smaller, but their real-world size does not change. Rulers show the new measurement units.

Working with Building Plan Layouts

Use the following procedure to create a floor plan:

Step 1: Select the File tab to open the Backstage view.

Step 2: Select New.

Step 3: Search for Floor Plans.

Step 4: Select Floor Plan.

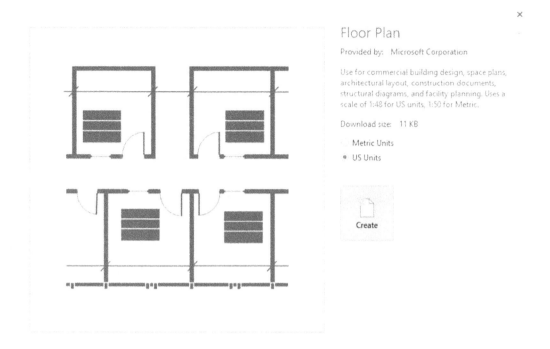

Floor Plan

Provided by: Microsoft Corporation

Use for commercial building design, space plans, architectural layout, construction documents, structural diagrams, and facility planning. Uses a scale of 1:48 for US units, 1:50 for Metric.

Download size: 11 KB

- Metric Units
- • US Units

[Create]

Step 5: Use the Walls, Shells, and Structure shapes to create the basic exterior wall structure, interior walls, and any other structure elements, doors, and windows. Then you can add electrical symbols and dimension lines.

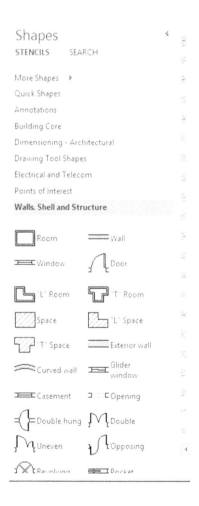

Use the following procedure to insert a CAD floor plan:

Step 1: Create a new floor plan (as in the previous procedure).

Step 2: Select the Insert tab from the Ribbon.

Step 3: Select CAD Drawing.

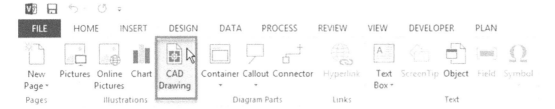

Step 4: Navigate to the AutoCAD Drawing you want to insert and select Open.

Step 5: To accept the size and location of the CAD drawing, select OK. You can resize it, change its scale, or move it once it is in the drawing. You can lock the layer that contains the CAD drawing so that it is not accidentally changed.

In this chapter, we'll look at using data in your drawings. First, we'll look at how you can use data with graphics to create a professional diagram that combines textual and graphical elements to illustrate your data. Then, you'll learn how to use the Data Selector Wizard to connect your drawing to an external data source. You'll learn how to apply a data graphic to your drawing. Finally, you'll learn how to edit the data graphic to get it looking just like you want.

About Data Graphics

Data graphics can enhance your shapes to show data the shapes contain. You can connect your drawings to data, either by entering the data in Visio, or by connecting your drawing to an external data source. Once your drawing is connected to a data source, you can add data graphics to your drawing either by adding new shapes based on the data, or by applying the data to existing shapes. A data graphic combines the following elements:

- Text

- Data bar

- Icons

- Color

Using the Data Selector Wizard

Use the following procedure to create a new data connection to a blank drawing:

Step 1: Select the Data tab from the Ribbon.

Step 2: Select Link Data to Shapes to start the Data Selector Wizard.

Step 3: Select the type of data connection you want to use. In this example, we'll select Microsoft Office Excel workbook. Select Next.

Step 4: Select Browse to locate the Excel workbook you want to use. Locate the file and select Open.

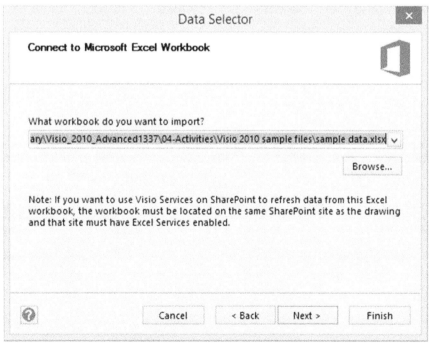

Step 5: Select Next.

Step 6: This screen of the Data Selector Wizard allows you to customize which part of the workbook to use. You can select a different sheet from the drop down list (if applicable), choose the Select Custom Range button to customize which part of the workbook is used, or check or clear the First row of data contains column headings box as applicable. Select Next to continue.

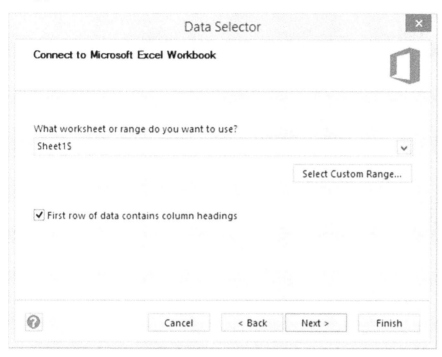

Step 7: The next screen of the Data Selector Wizard allows you to customize which columns and rows to include. Choose the Select Columns button to choose which columns to include.

Step 8: Check or clear the columns as desired. Select OK to return to the Data Selector Wizard.

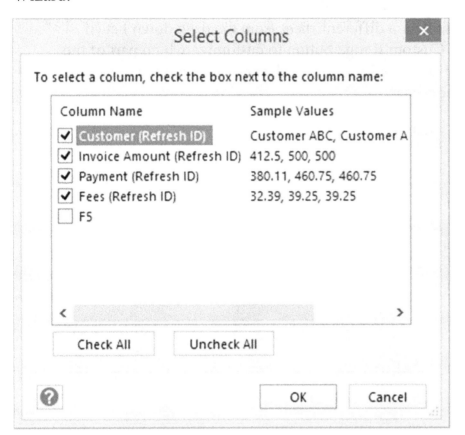

Step 9: Choose the Select Rows button to filter the rows to include.

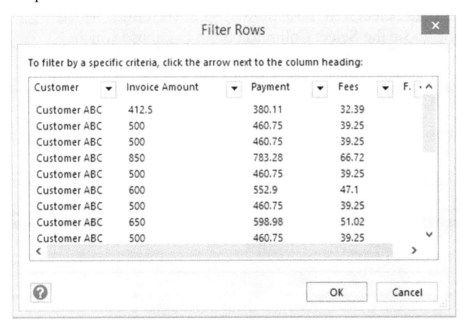

Step 10: Each column heading has an arrow next to it. Select an option from one or more drop down list to filter the rows to include in your data connection. Select OK to return to the Data Selector Wizard.

Step 11: Here is the modified Data Selector Wizard screen. Select Next to continue.

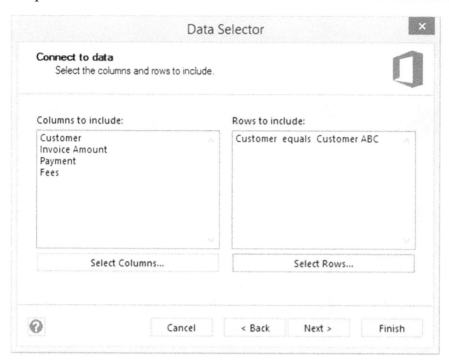

Step 12: The next screen identifies the unique identifier for refresh purposes. Since this data doesn't have a unique identifier, we'll choose the second option. Select Next to continue.

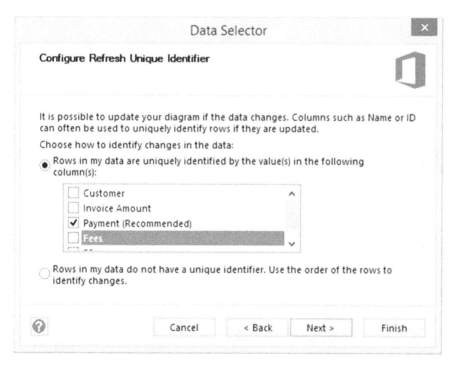

Step 13: The Wizard displays a notification that the data was successfully imported. Select Finish.

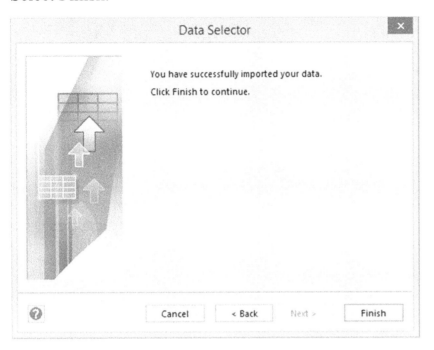

The External Data window opens with your imported data.

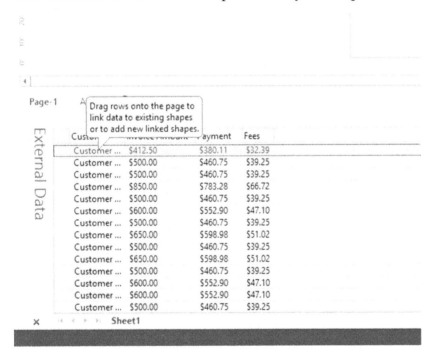

Applying Data Graphics

Use the following procedure to drag a data row onto the drawing:

Step 1: Drag a row from the External Data window onto the drawing. Visio automatically applies the shape you selected in the Shapes window.

Step 2: Notice the chain icon in the External Data window, indicating that the row is linked to a shape.

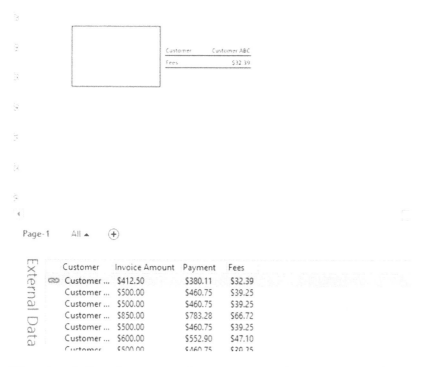

Use the following procedure to open the Data Graphic task pane:

Step 1: Select Task Pane from the View tab on the Ribbon.

Use the following procedure to apply a different data graphic to a shape with data:

Step 1: Select the shape in the drawing.

Step 2: Select the Data tab from the Ribbon.

Step 3: Select Data Graphics.

Step 4: Select the data graphic from the Available Data Graphics gallery. You can see a live preview of the new data graphic before you apply it.

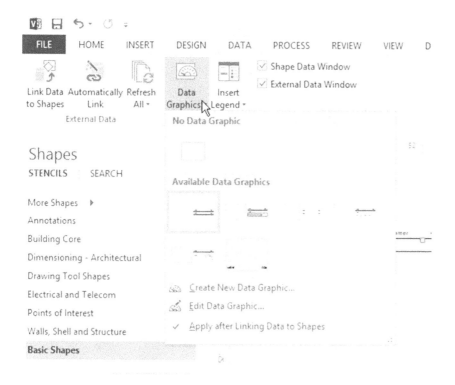

Editing Data Graphics

Use the following procedure to edit a Data Graphic:

Step 1: Right-click on the shape and select Data from the context menu. Select Edit Data Graphic.

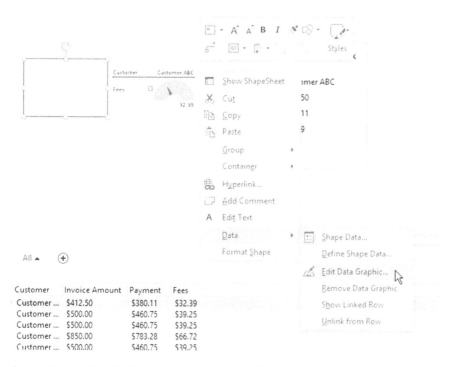

Step 2: In the Edit Data Graphic dialog box, you can choose a new data field to display for the items already added to this data graphic by choosing a new field from the drop down lists. You can also change the display position or change the display options.

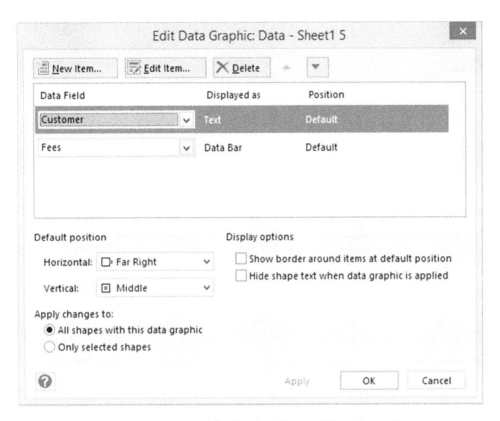

Here's what the data graphic looks like with a few changes.

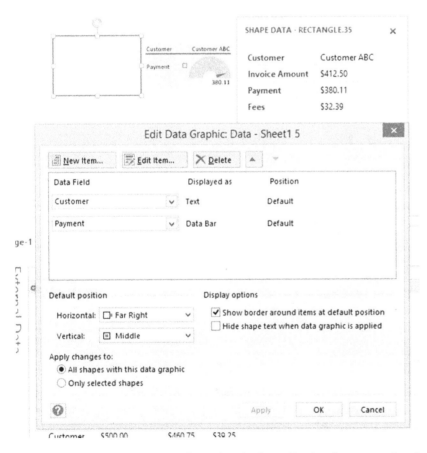

It's still not what I'm after. So let's edit the item to further refine it.

Step 3: Select the item that you want to modify and select Edit Item. Let's start with the Text item.

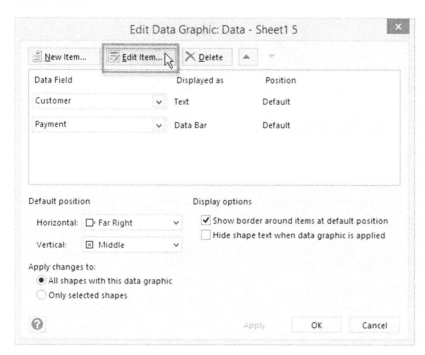

Step 4: The Edit Text dialog box opens to help determine how to format the text. You can select a new column from the Data field drop down list, if desired. However, I want to leave it as Customer.

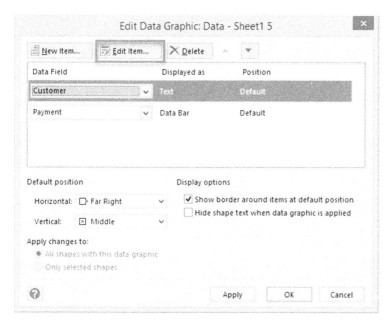

Step 5: Let's select a new Callout format from the drop down list.

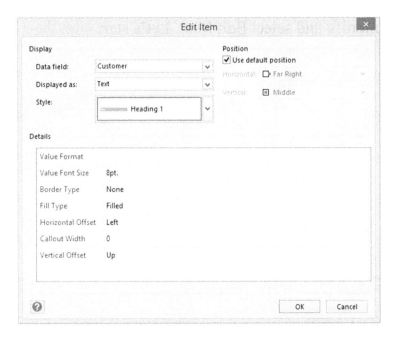

Step 6: You can customize the Callout position, or just leave the Use default position check box checked.

Step 7: In the Details area, you can customize the data graphic further. We can leave the defaults for now.

Step 8: Select OK to save your changes to the Text item.

Step 9: Now let's adjust the data bar part of the graphic. Select the Data Bar item and select Edit Item.

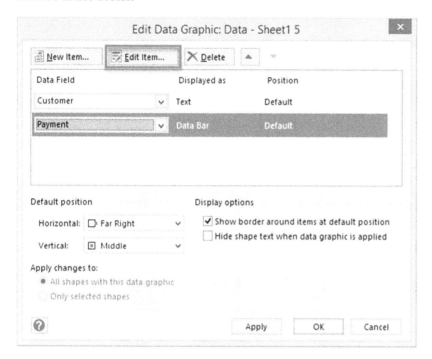

Step 10: The Edit Data Bar dialog box opens to help you format the data graphic. It works in a similar way to the Edit Text dialog box. Just select the Data field and Callout format from the drop down lists. You can leave the defaults on everything else. I want to select the Speedometer data bar format. Select OK to continue.

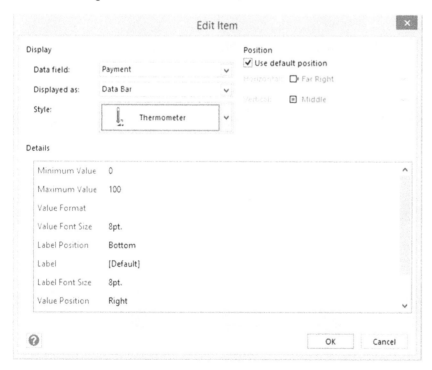

Step 11: Select OK to close the Edit Data Graphic dialog box.

Here is the updated data graphic.

Use the following procedure to add a new item to the data graphic:

Step 1: Open the Edit Data Graphic dialog box as you did in the previous procedure.

Step 2: Select New Item.

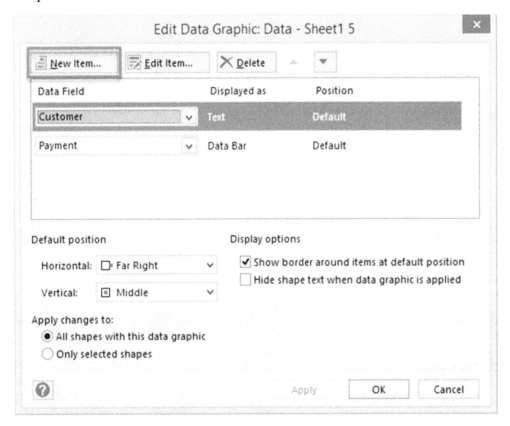

Step 3: The New Item dialog box opens. Choose a Data field from the drop down list.

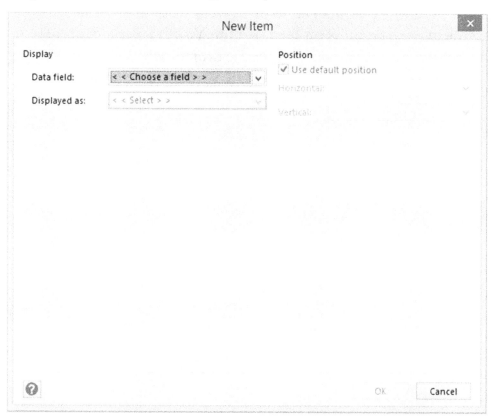

Step 4: Choose an element type from the Displayed as drop down list. In this example, we'll choose Icon set.

Step 5: The New Icon Set dialog box opens to help you format the data graphic. It works in a similar way to the Edit Text and Edit Data Bar dialog boxes. Just select a Style from the drop down list. You can leave the defaults on the position. You'll need to add rules for the icons that you want to use. Select an option from the drop down list (or select [Not Used]) and enter a value, an expression or a date. Select OK when you have finished.

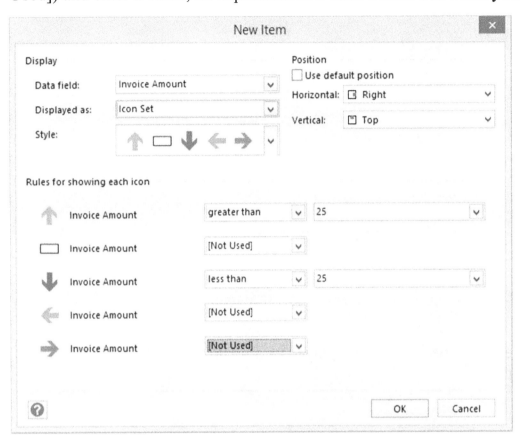

Step 6: Select Apply to preview the changes. Select OK to close the Edit Data Graphic dialog box.

Data Graphic Legends

Use the following procedure to insert a data graphic legend:

Step 1: Select the Data tab from the Ribbon.

Step 2: Select Insert Legend.

Step 3: Select the type of legend you want to use.

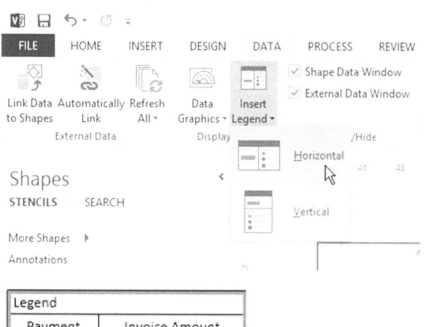

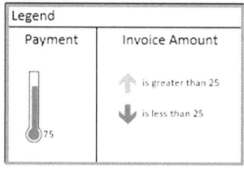

Chapter 8 – The ShapeSheet

In this chapter, we'll take a look at the ShapeSheet. You'll learn how to view the ShapeSheet and how to modify ShapeSheet data. You'll also learn how to use formulas in the ShapeSheet.

Viewing the ShapeSheet

Use the following procedure to view the ShapeSheet

First, you'll need to display the Developer tab, if it isn't already displayed.

Step 1: Select the File tab to open the Backstage View.

Step 2: Select Options.

Step 3: Select the Advanced category.

Step 4: Scroll down to the General section.

Step 5: Check the Run in Developer mode box.

Step 6: Select OK.

If the Developer tab is already displayed, start here.

Step 7: If you want to display the ShapeSheet for the shape or the page, make sure you select the desired shape first or make the page you want to show active.

Step 8: Select the Developer tab.

Step 9: Select Show ShapeSheet.

Step 10: Select Shape, Page, or Document.

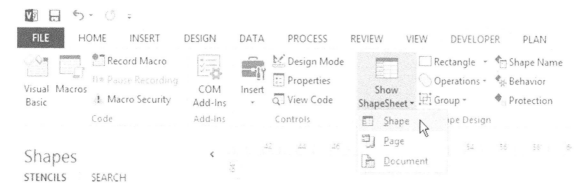

The following diagram shows the ShapeSheet Tools Design tab.

If you select a shape before opening the ShapeSheet, the ShapeSheet shows data for only the selected shape.

The Shape ShapeSheet data includes values for the shape, the user-defined cells (or data), the connection points, Geometry data, Protection data, Miscellaneous, the Line Format data, the Fill format data, the Character, Paragraph, Tab and Text block formatting, Events, Image Properties, Glue Info and Shape Layout.

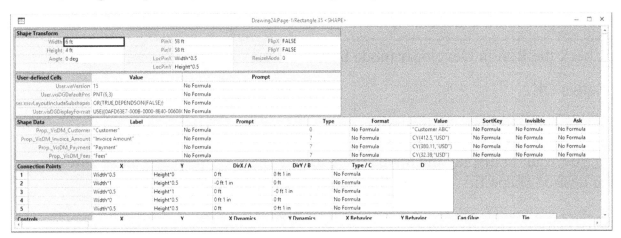

The Page ShapeSheet data includes values for the page properties, the Page layout, the Rule & grid properties and the Print properties.

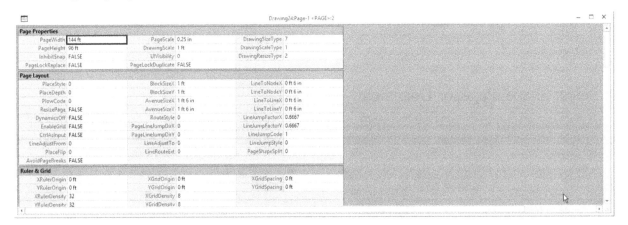

The Document ShapeSheet includes values for the document properties and user-defined cells.

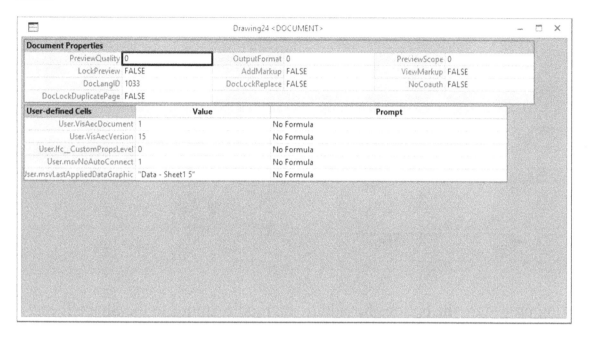

Modifying ShapeSheet Data

In addition to modifying values in the ShapeSheet data fields, you can also perform the following tasks:

- Add a New Row (for some sections)

- Add a Section

- Change a Row Type

- Delete a Row

- Delete a Section

There are additional ShapeSheet tasks, depending on the type of shape or section you are working with.

Use the following procedure to modify a shape by using the ShapeSheet:

Step 1: Select the shape you want to change.

Step 2: Display the ShapeSheet for the selected shape.

Step 3: Enter new values in the desired fields. In this example, the width and height have been changed. You can also use the Pin values to change the position of the shape.

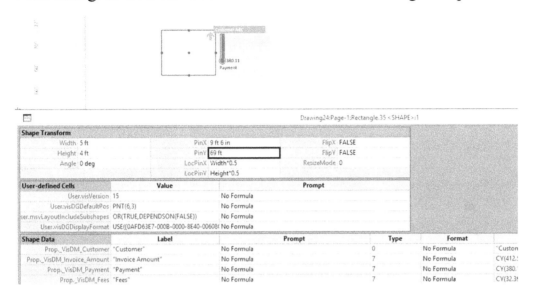

Use the following procedure the options for additional modifications to the ShapeSheet:

Step 1: Right-click in the ShapeSheet to see the options.

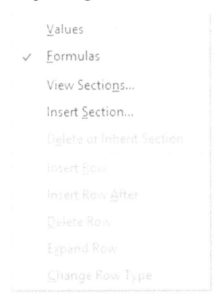

Investigate the options (View Sections, Insert Section, Delete Section, Insert Row, Insert Row After, Delete Row, Expand Row and Change Row Type), depending on the level of the students and the time available. These options are also available from the ShapeSheet Tools Design tab.

Using a Formula in the ShapeSheet

Use the following procedure to enter a formula into a ShapeSheet cell:

Step 1: Click in the ShapeSheet window to make it active.

Step 2: Make sure that formulas are displayed. To check, select Formulas from the ShapeSheet Tools Design tab on the Ribbon.

Step 3: Place your cursor in the cell where you want the formula.

Step 4: Use the Formula bar to enter your formula.

Step 5: Select Accept (or press the Enter key) to complete the formula. Notice the cell may contain the result of the formula instead of the formula itself.

You can also use the Edit Formula tool from the ShapeSheet Tools Design tab.

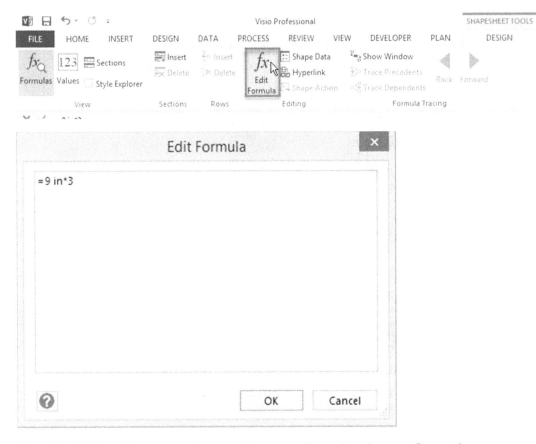

Use the following procedure to insert a function into a formula:

Step 1: Double-click the cell where you want to use a formula with a function.

Step 2: Place the insertion point where you want to paste the function.

Step 3: Type = to begin your formula.

Step 4: Type the first few letters of the function you want to use.

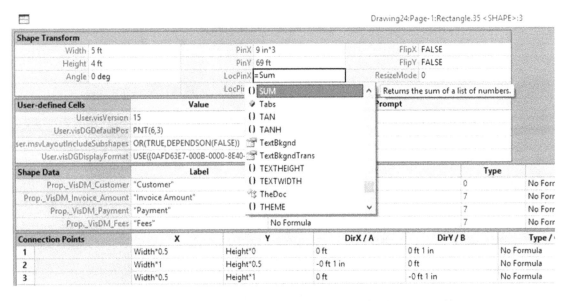

Step 5: Select the Function from the quick list under your cell.

Step 6: Visio helps you with the function arguments.

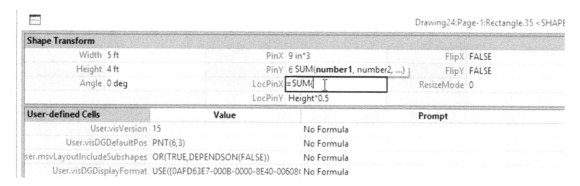

Step 7: Include the appropriate arguments for the function. You can enter them by typing them, by selecting appropriate ShapeSheet cells, or by using the NAME function to select ShapeSheet cells.

Step 8: Press the ENTER key to accept changes to the formula. Or you can press ESC to cancel the changes.

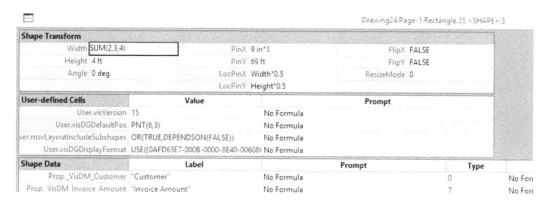

Additional Titles

The Technical Skill Builder series of books covers a variety of technical application skills. For the availability of titles please see https://www.silvercitypublications.com/shop/. Note the Master Class volume contains the Essentials, Advanced, and Expert (when available) editions.

Current Titles

Microsoft Excel 2013 Essentials

Microsoft Excel 2013 Advanced

Microsoft Excel 2013 Expert

Microsoft Excel 2013 Master Class

Microsoft Word 2013 Essentials

Microsoft Word 2013 Advanced

Microsoft Word 2013 Expert

Microsoft Word 2013 Master Class

Microsoft Project 2010 Essentials

Microsoft Project 2010 Advanced

Microsoft Project 2010 Expert

Microsoft Project 2010 Master Class

Microsoft Visio 2010 Essentials

Microsoft Visio 2010 Advanced

Microsoft Visio 2010 Master Class

www.ingramcontent.com/pod-product-compliance
Lightning Source LLC
Chambersburg PA
CBHW060200060326
40690CB00018B/4185